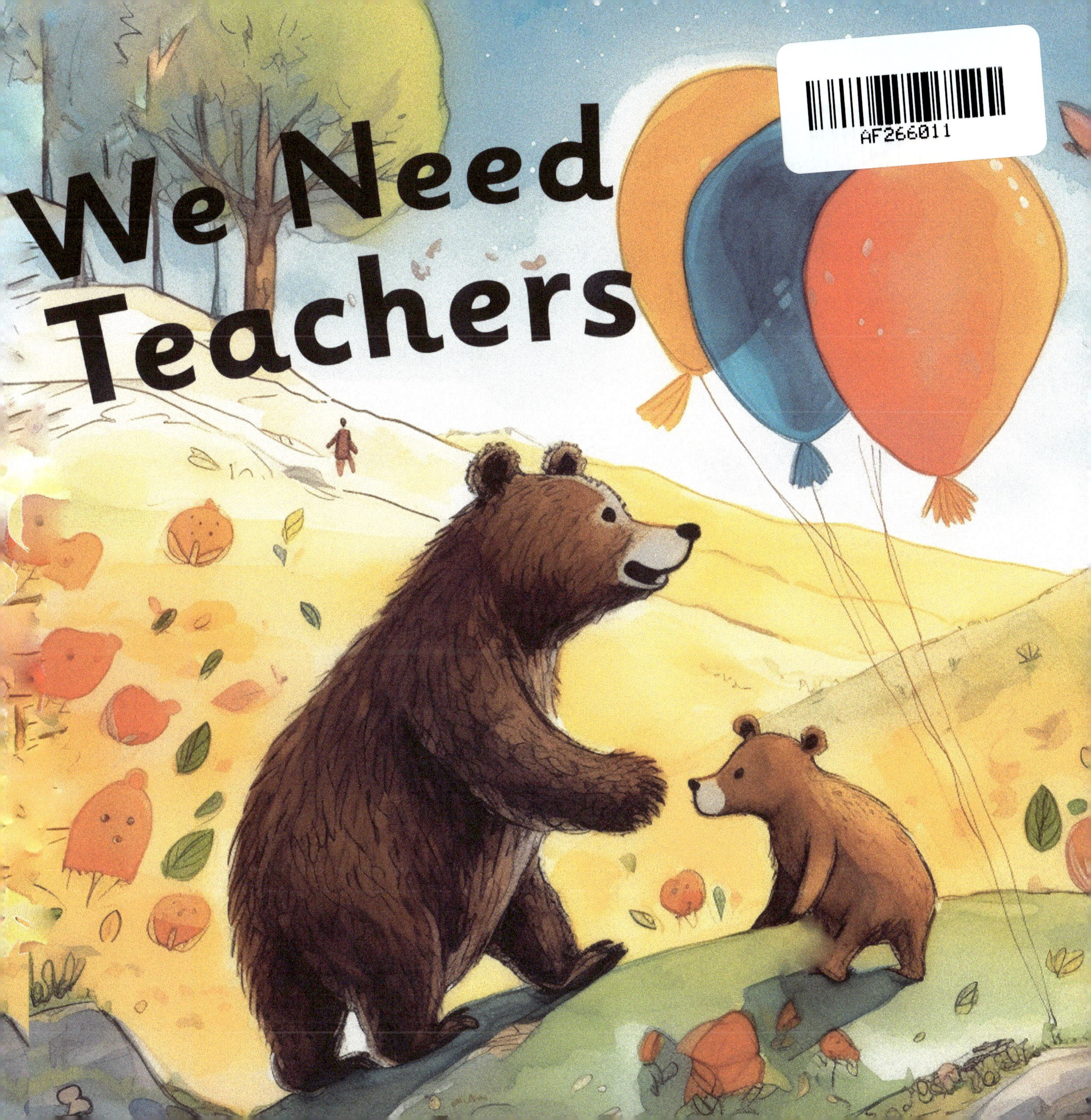

We Need Teachers

Get Free Coloring Book send a Mail After Purchase to
jonathanHillBooks@gmail.com

Dedicated to my sons, *Videl, Vishal & Valen*

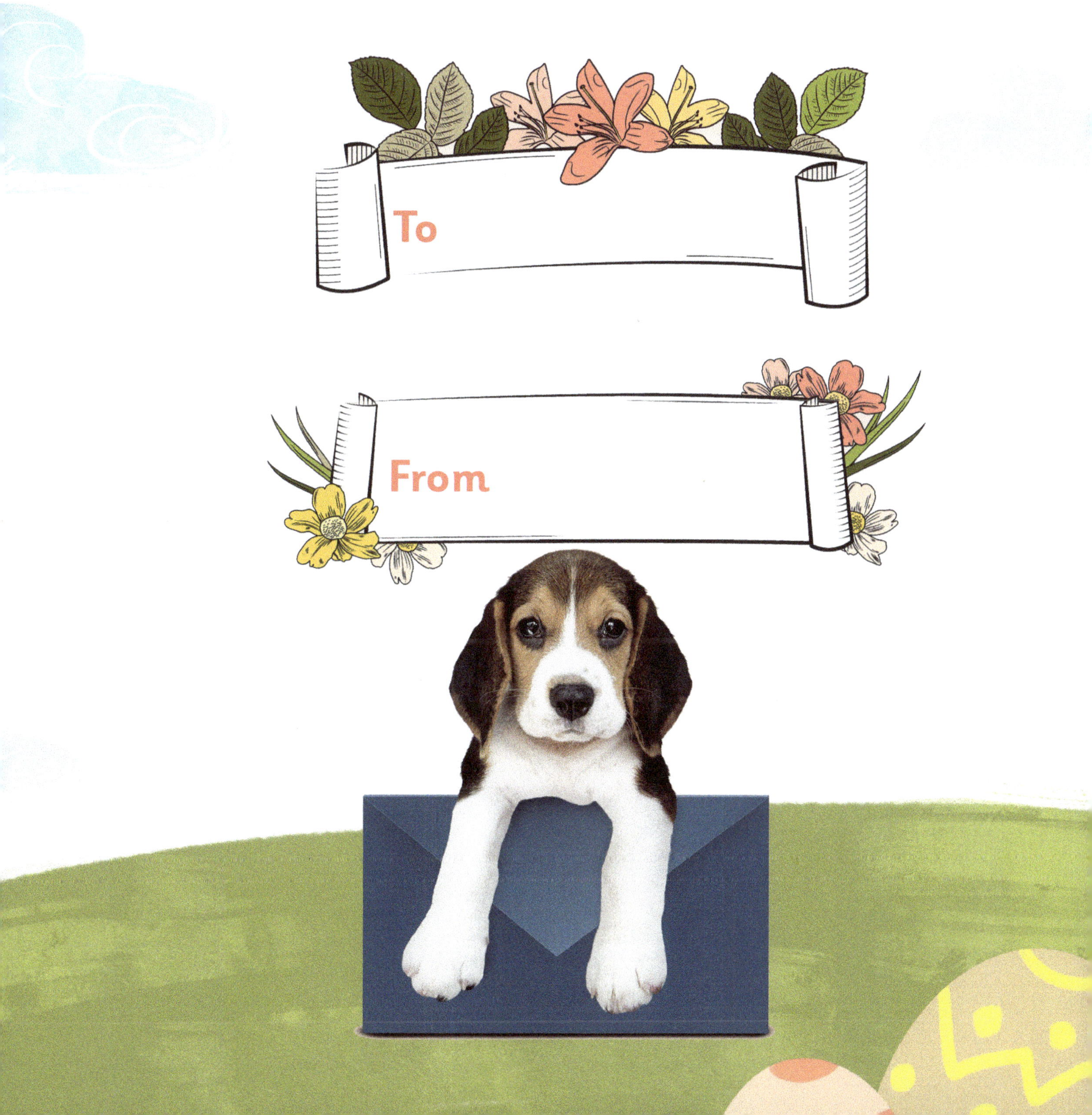
To

From

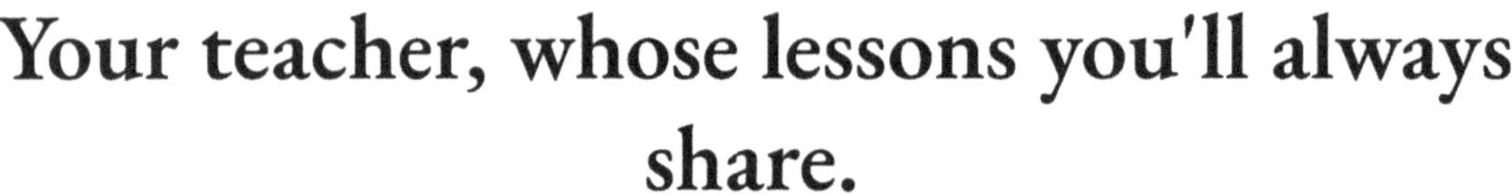

Who showed you how to think critically,
and to always question with care?
Who taught you to analyze, evaluate, and
never stop there?
Your teacher, whose lessons you'll always
share.

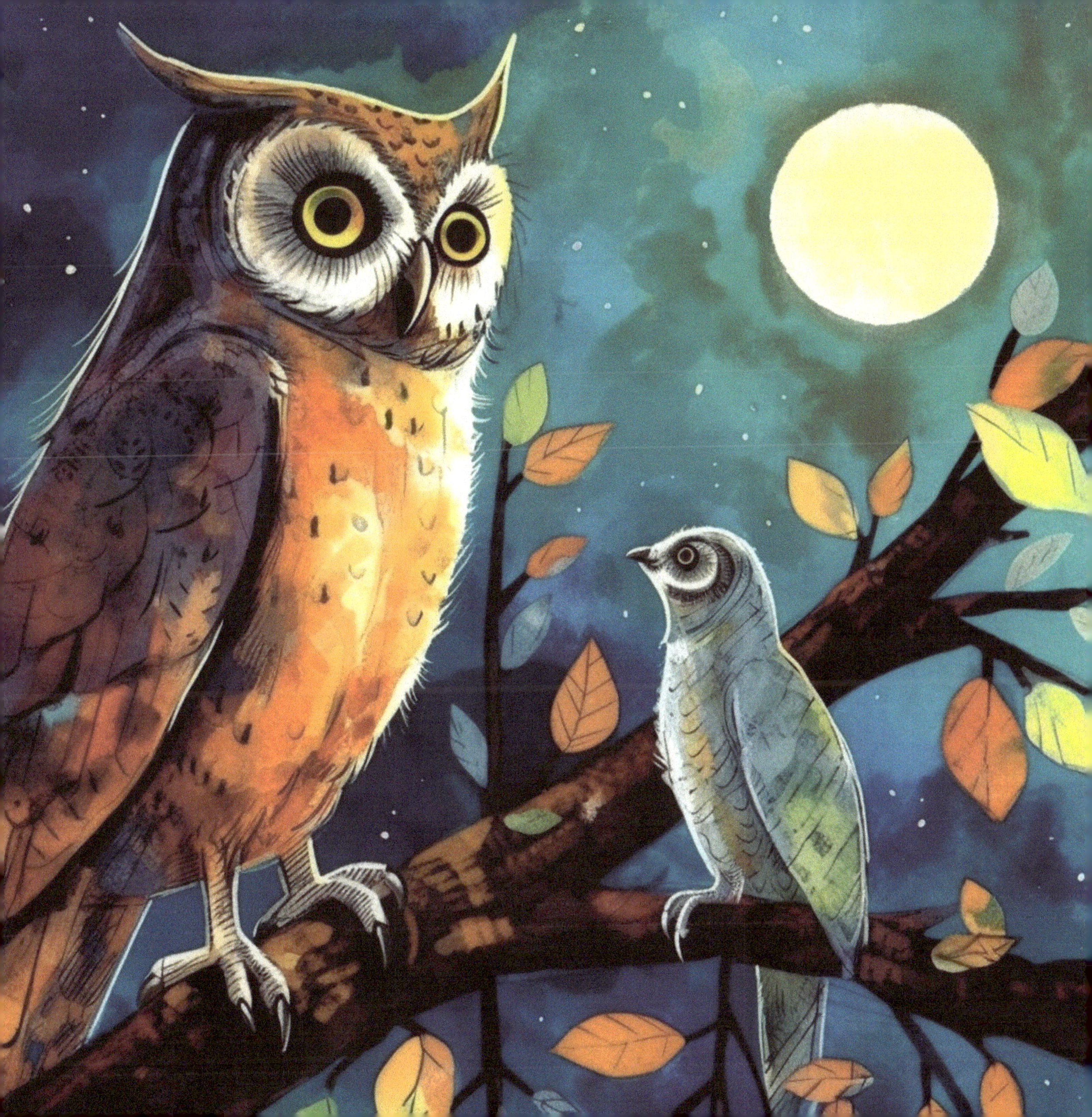

Who helped you see the beauty in art,
and to express yourself with creativity?
Who taught you the techniques and
styles, and to always pursue your
originality?
Your art teacher,
whose inspiration will never flee

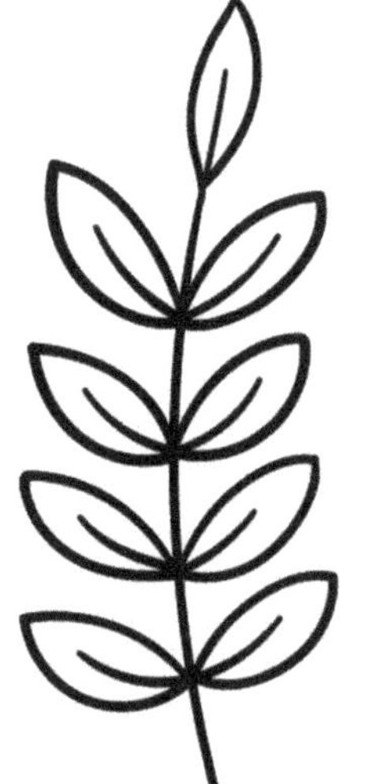

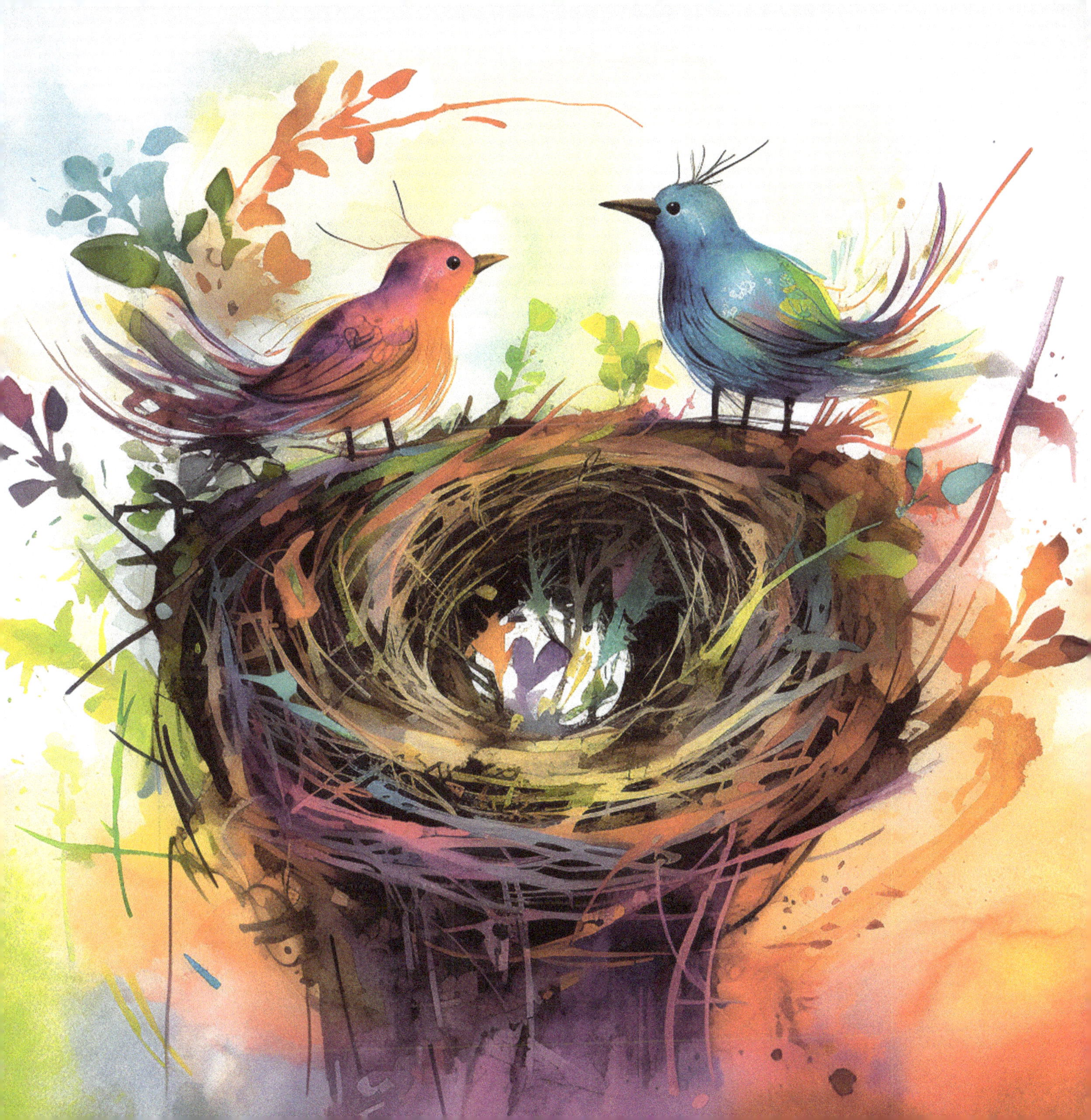

Who helped you understand the
mysteries of science, and to explore the
wonders of the world?
Who taught you to hypothesize,
experiment, and to always keep learning
unfurled?
Your science teacher,
whose passion for knowledge has forever
twirled.

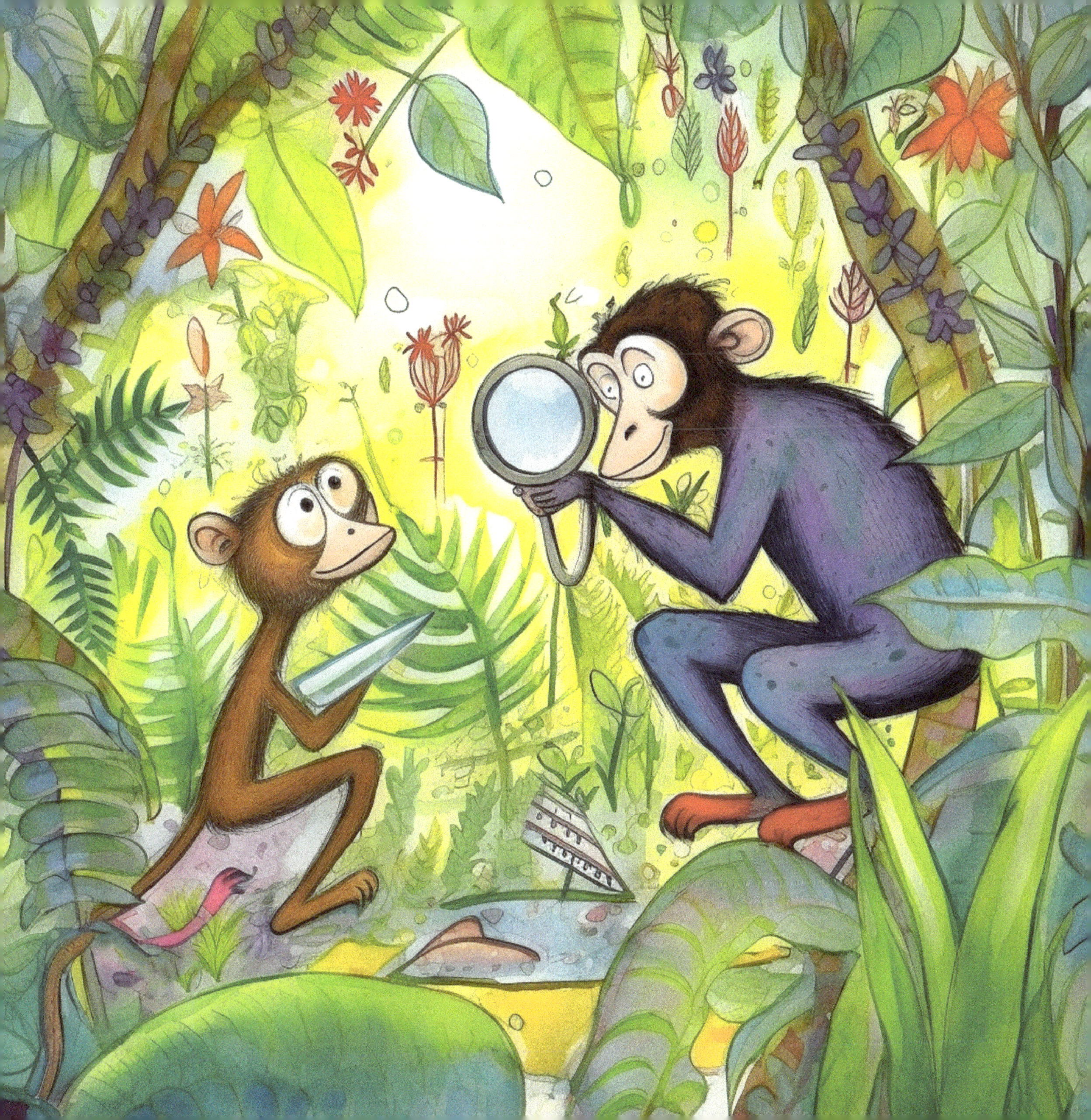

Who taught you to be a responsible
citizen, and to always do your part for
society?
Who showed you the value of
community service, and to always act
with propriety?
Your social studies teacher, whose
influence on your life will always be
mighty.

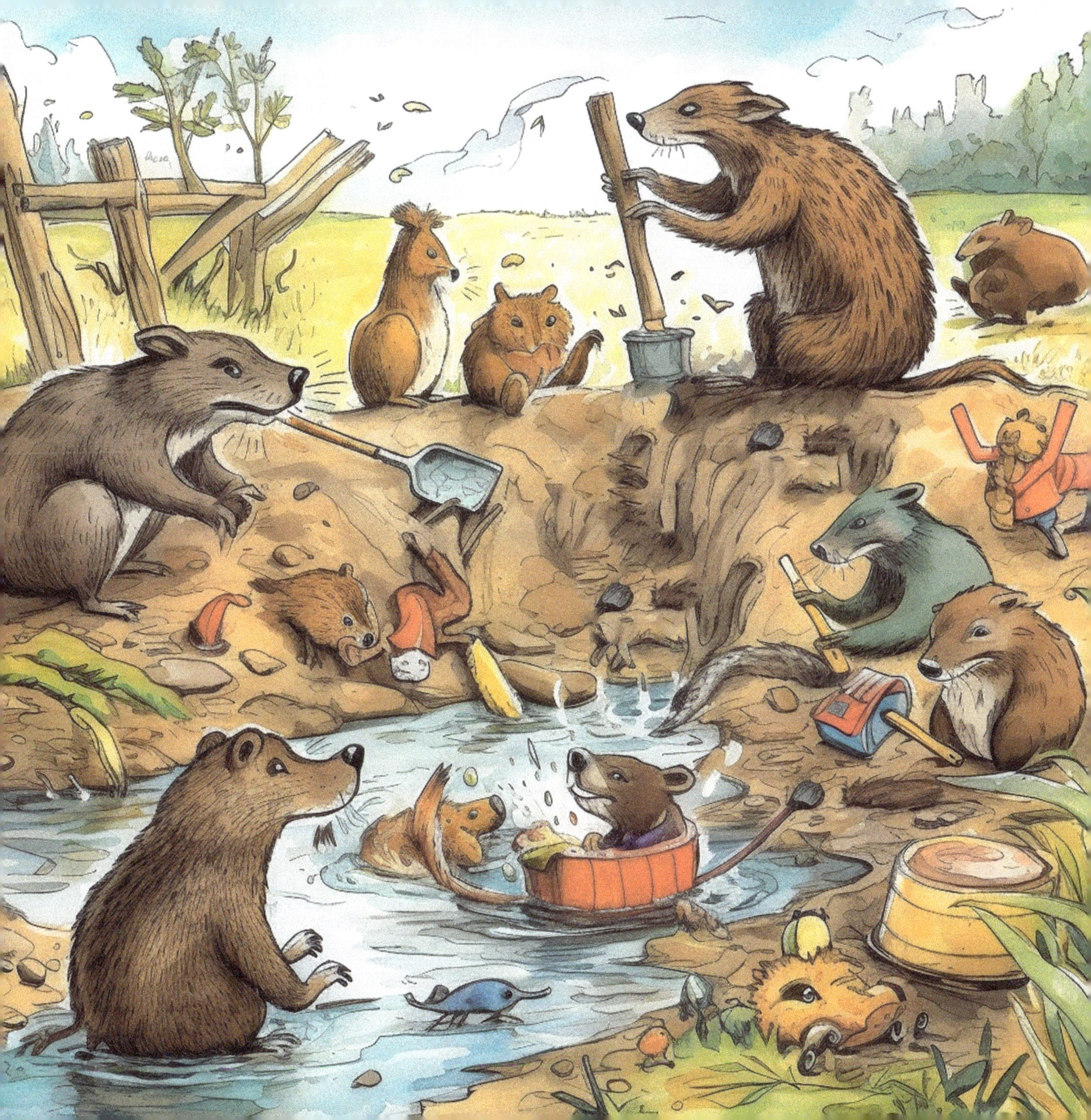

Who helped you understand different
cultures, and to embrace diversity with
an open mind?
Who taught you the value of respect and
inclusion, and to always be kind?
Your language teacher,
whose lessons will
forever be enshrined.

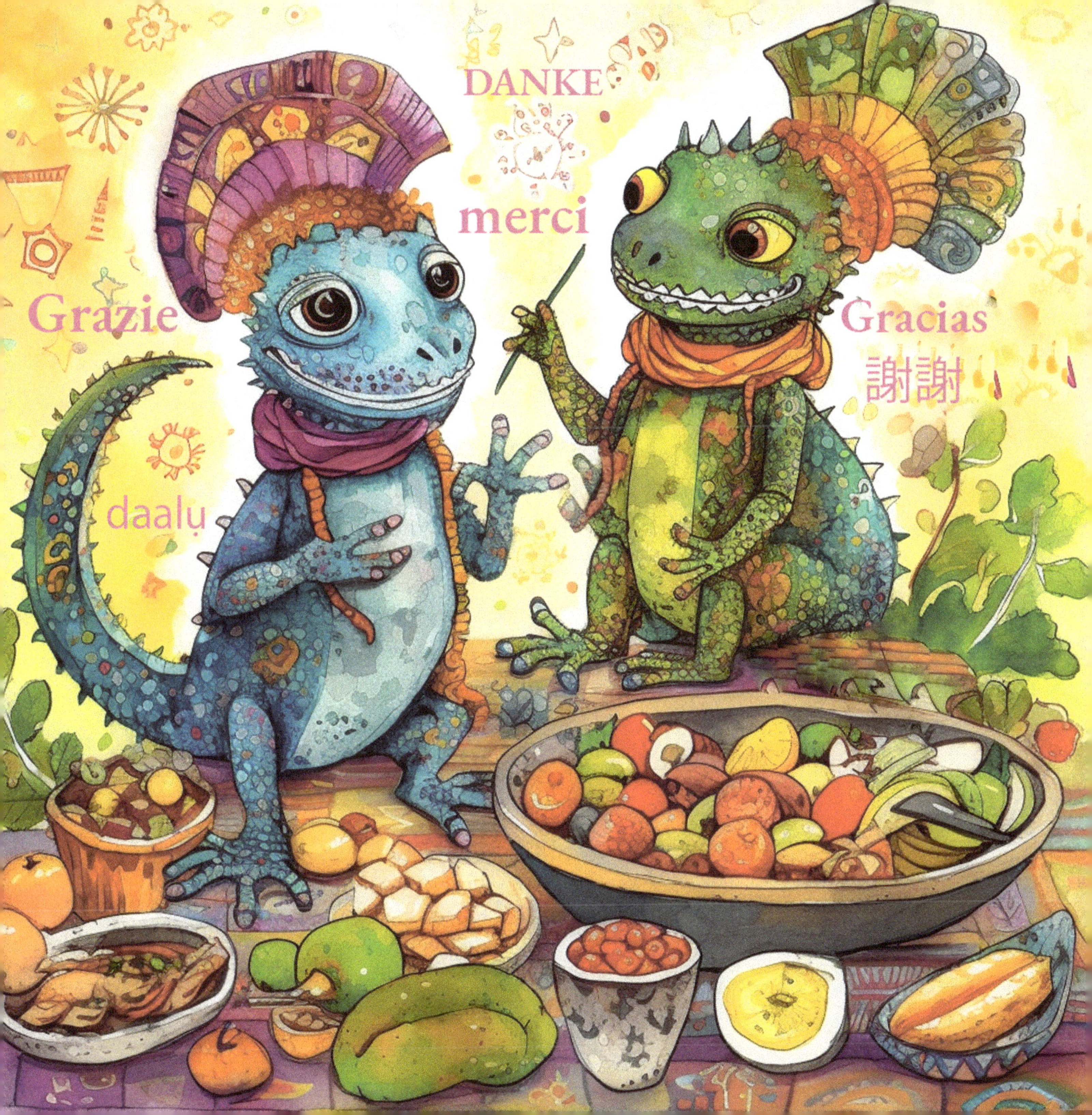

DANKE
merci
Grazie
Gracias
daalụ
謝謝

Who helped you learn to communicate
effectively, and to express yourself with
eloquence and grace?
Who taught you to listen, understand,
and to always seek to create a common
space?
Your English teacher,
whose wisdom
you'll forever embrace

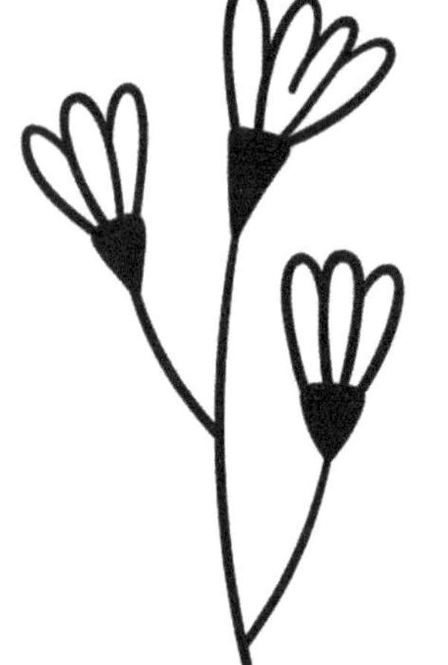

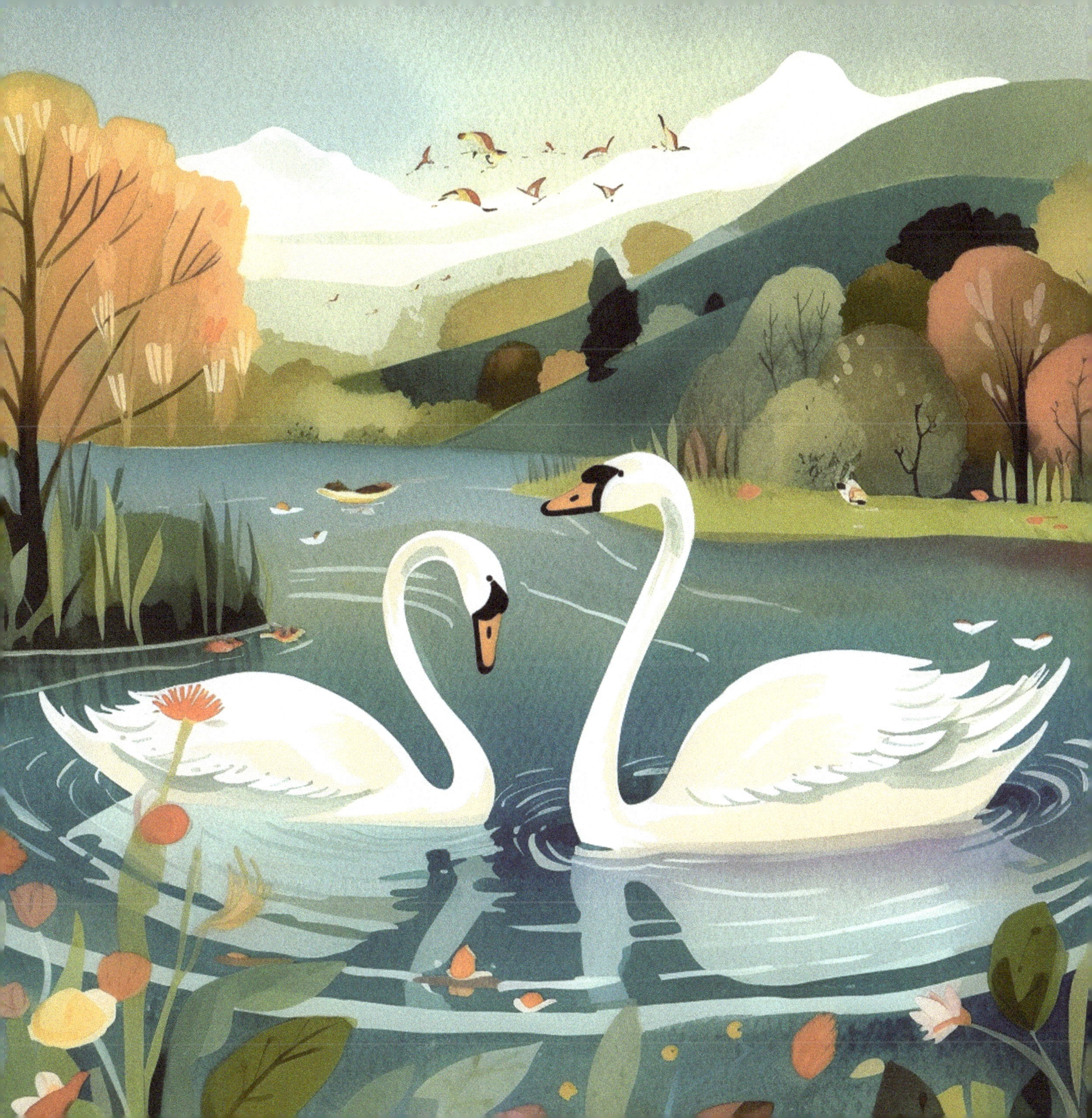

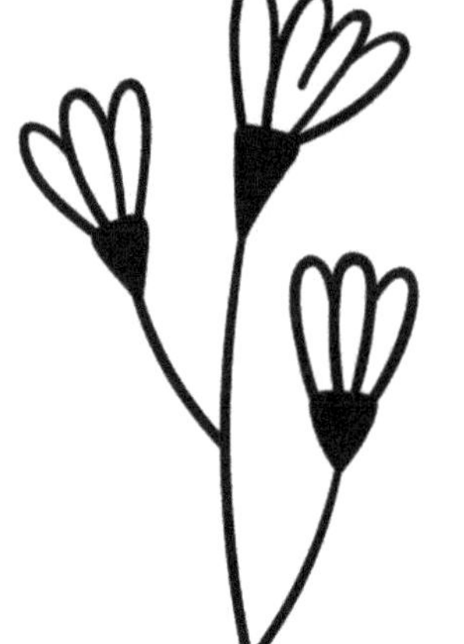

Who helped you discover your love of reading, and to find joy in books and stories?
Who showed you the power of imagination, and to always believe in life's glories?
Your reading teacher,
whose passion for words
always soars.

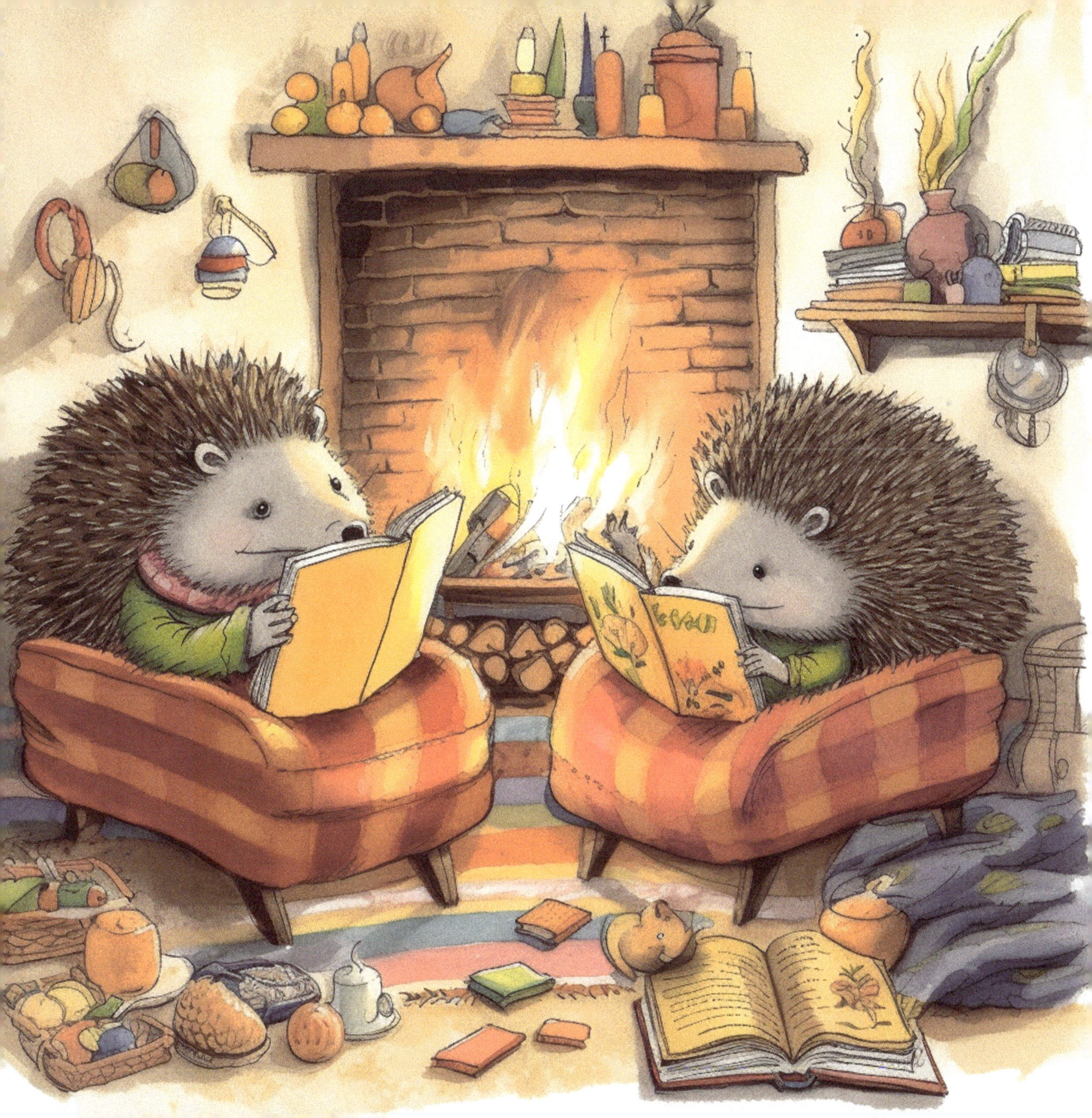

Who helped you believe in yourself, and
to never give up on your dreams?
Who showed you that failure is just a
step on the way, and that success is not as
far as it seems?
Your teacher, whose encouragement
forever beams

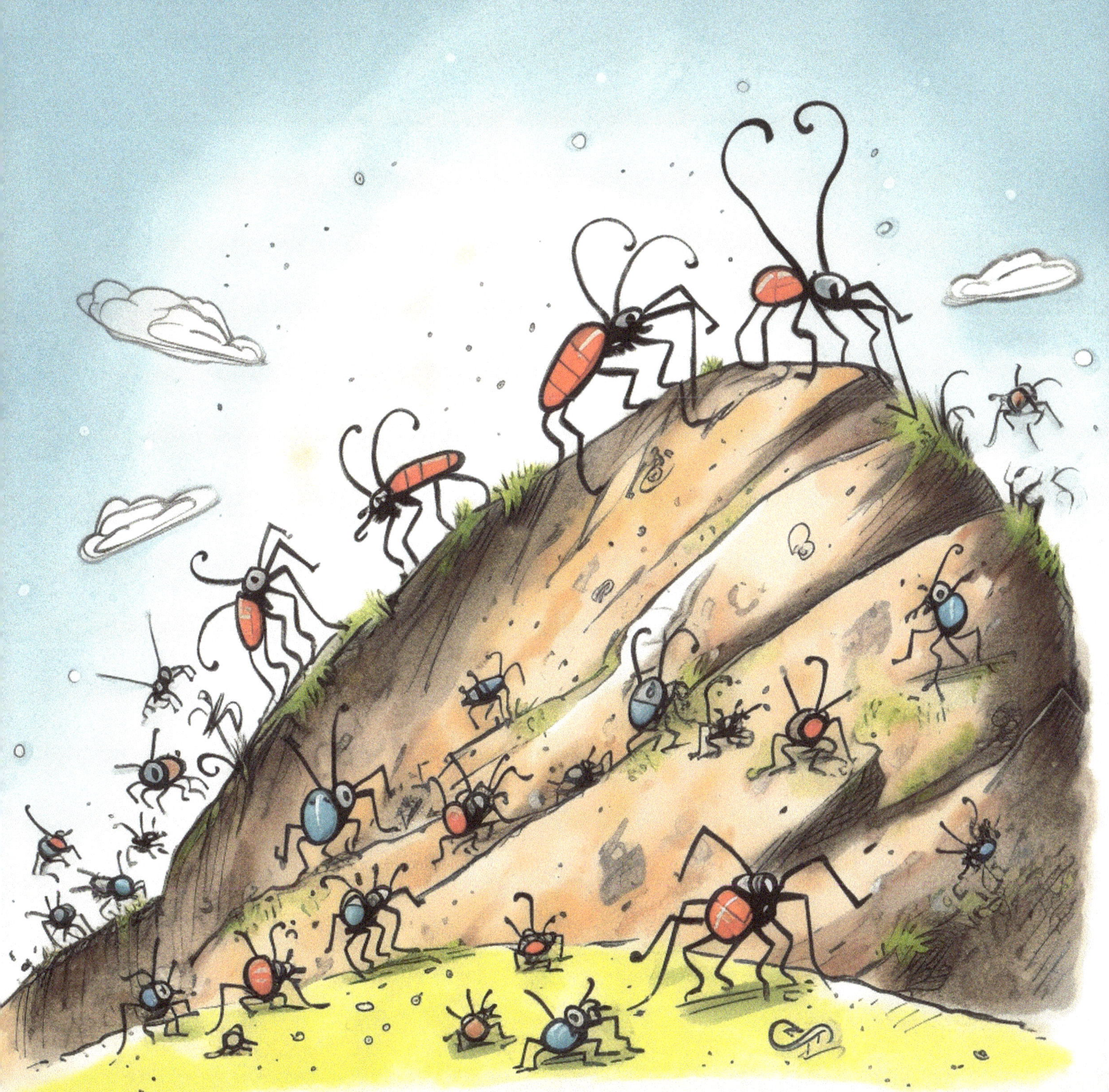

Who helped you realize your potential,
and to unlock the greatness within you?

Who taught you to aim high, and to
always pursue what's true?

Your teacher, whose belief in you will
always come through.

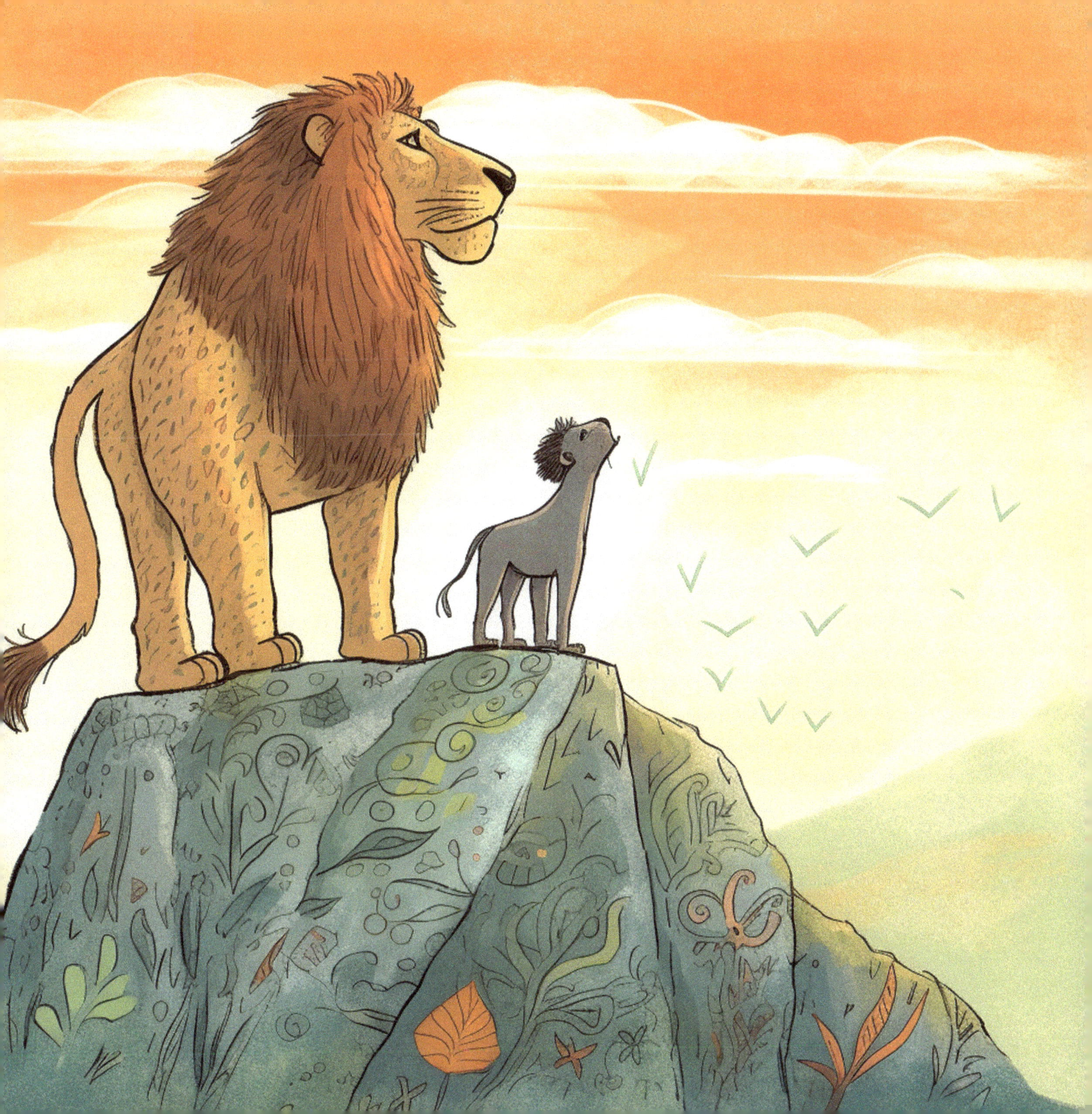

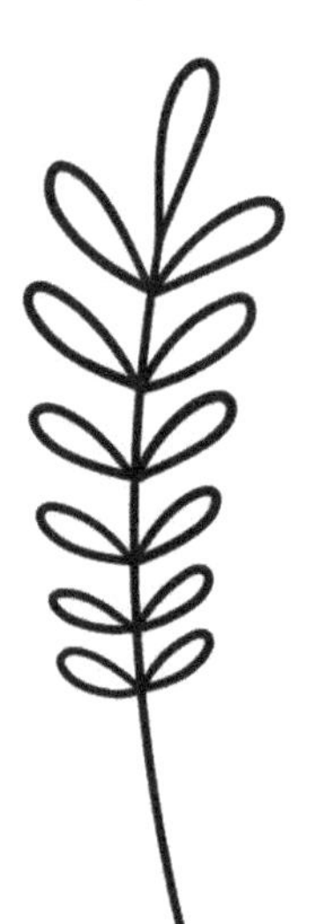

Learning to read and write,
adding and subtracting too,
a teacher's patience
and guidance helped us
learn something new

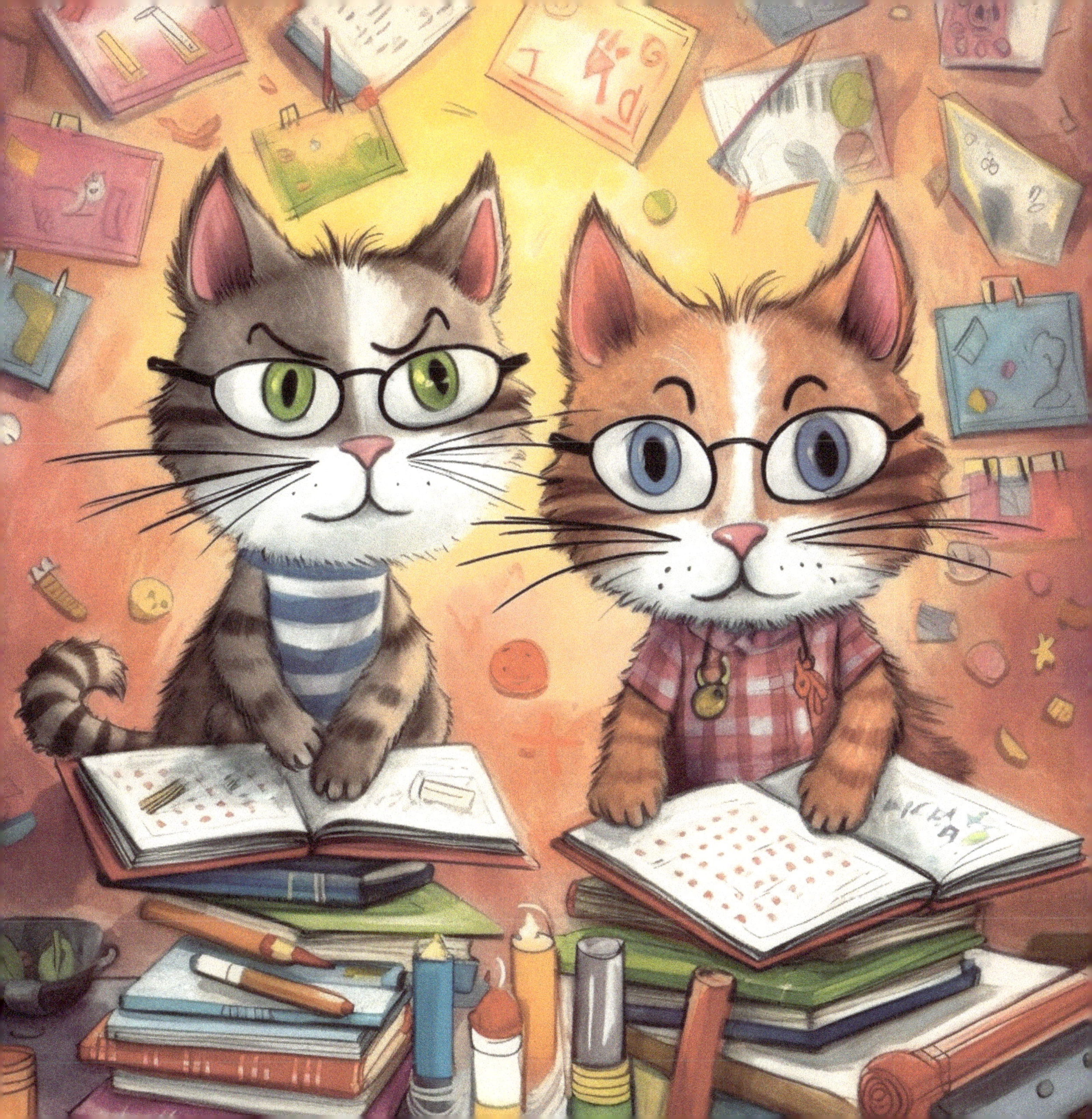

With their kindness and care,
teachers create a safe space
where we can grow
and learn at our own pace.

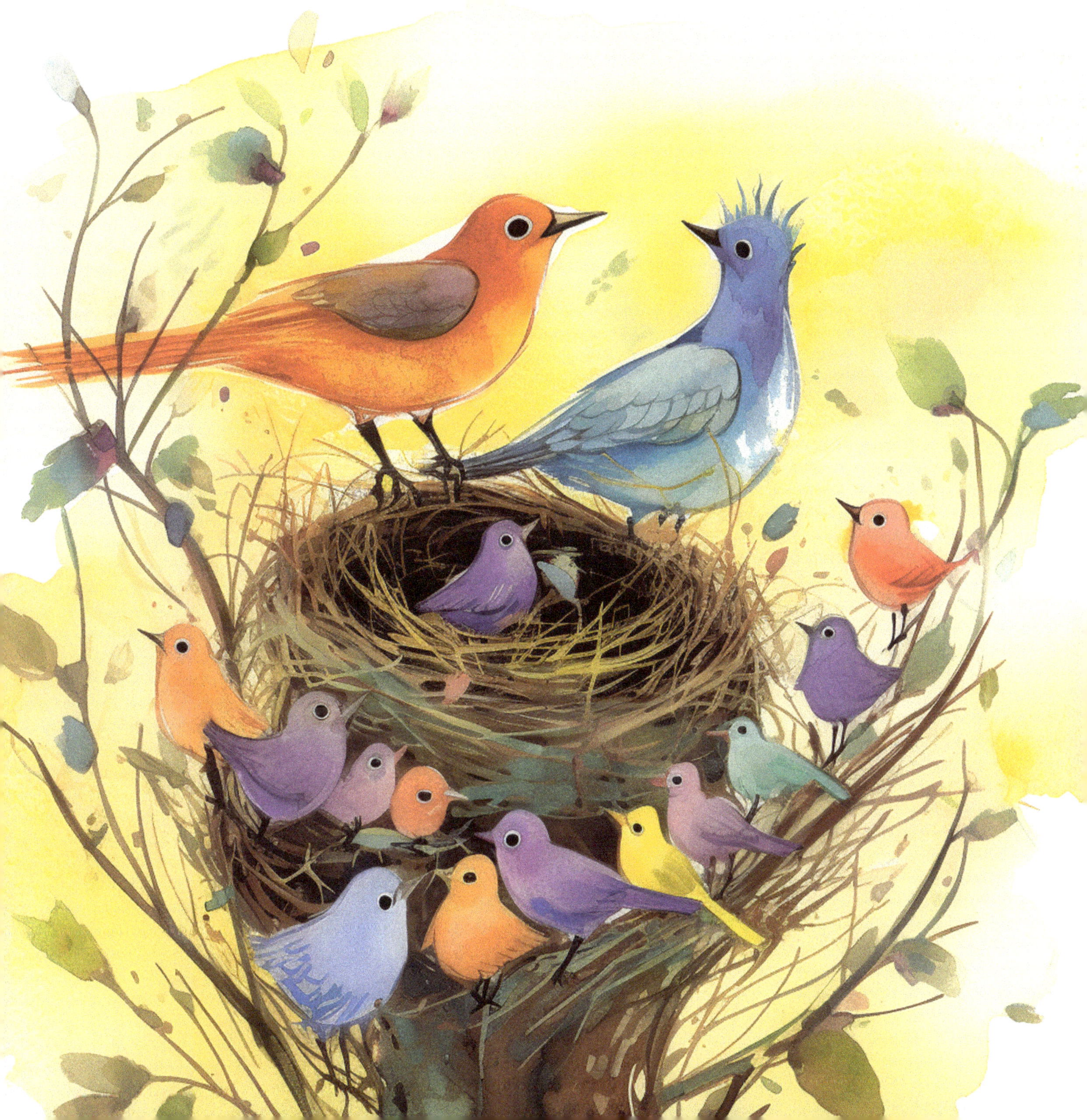

Teachers inspire us
to dream big,
to believe in ourselves,
and to pursue our passions
with all our might."

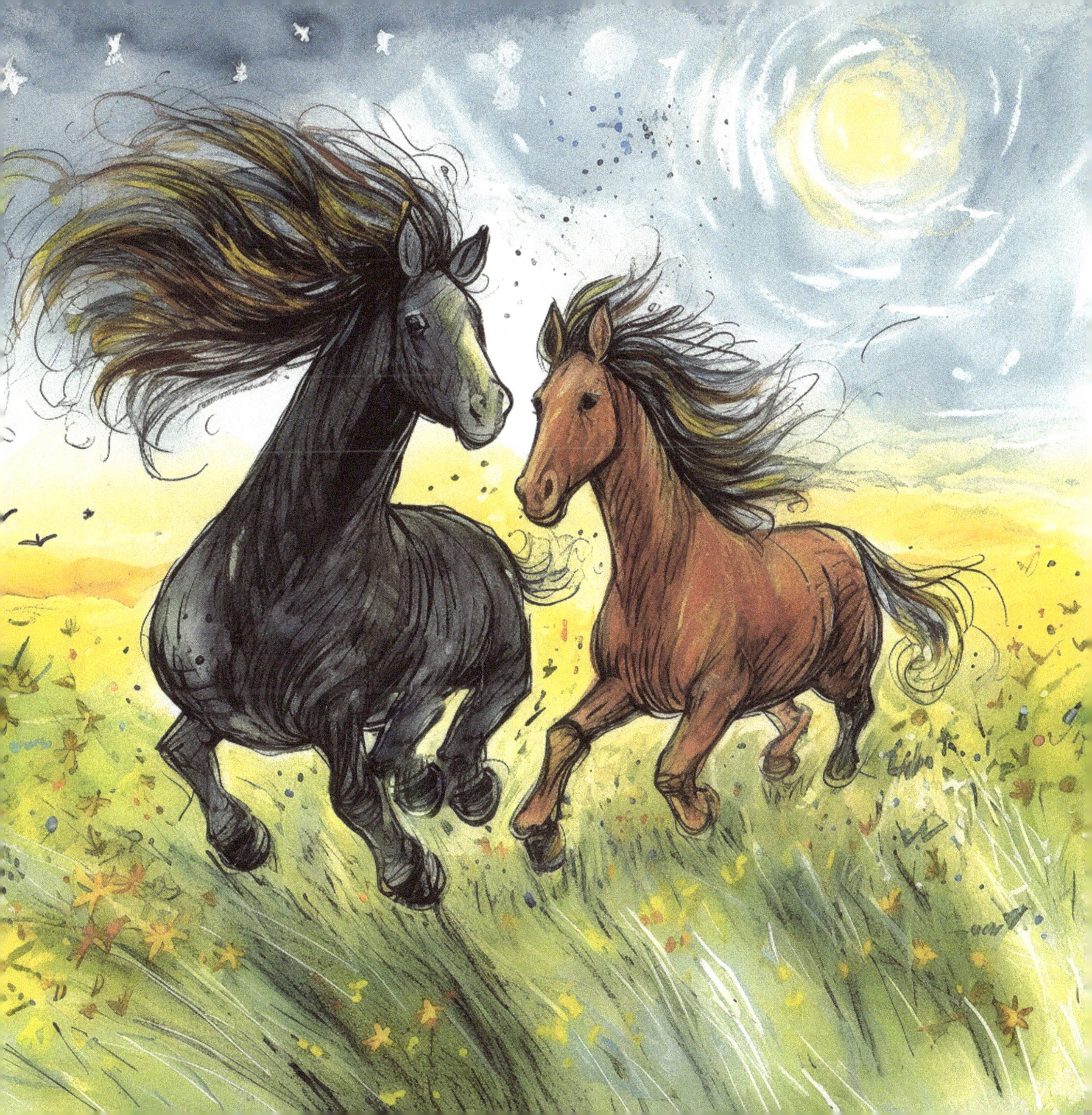

With their unwavering support
and encouragement,
teachers help us overcome
challenges and reach
our full potential.

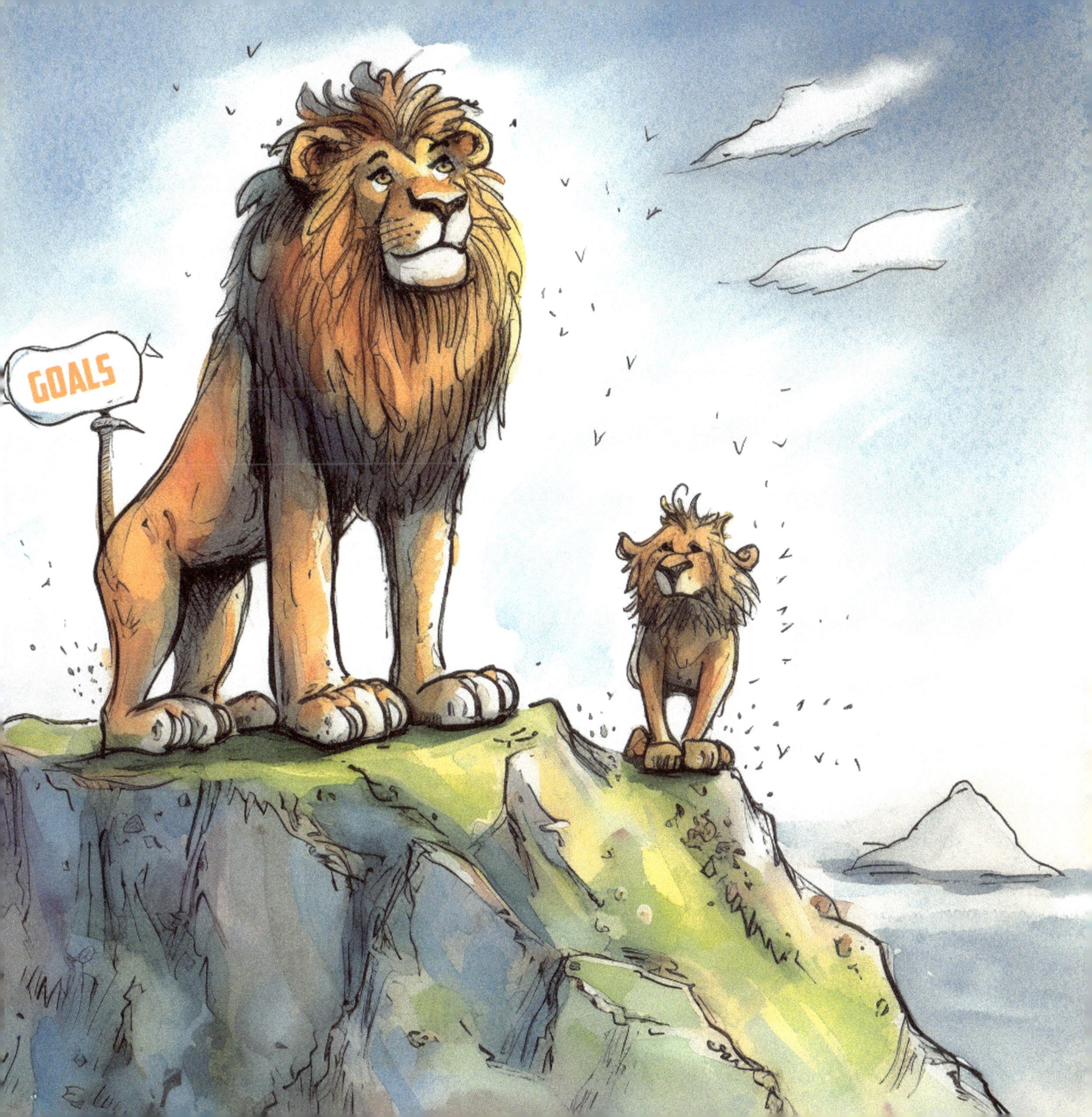
GOALS

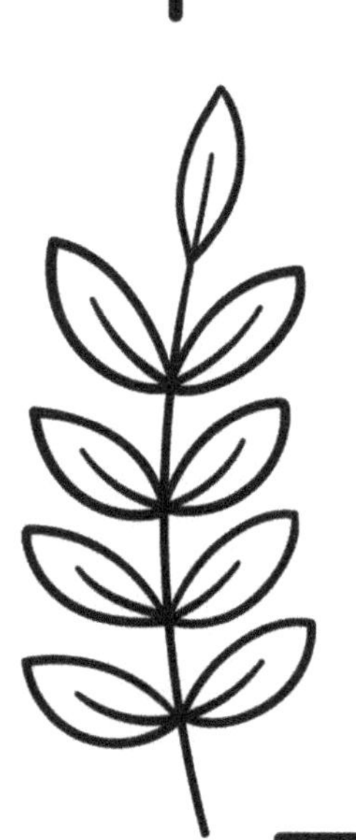

With their dedication
and commitment,
teachers help us overcome
obstacles and reach our goals,
no matter how big
or small.

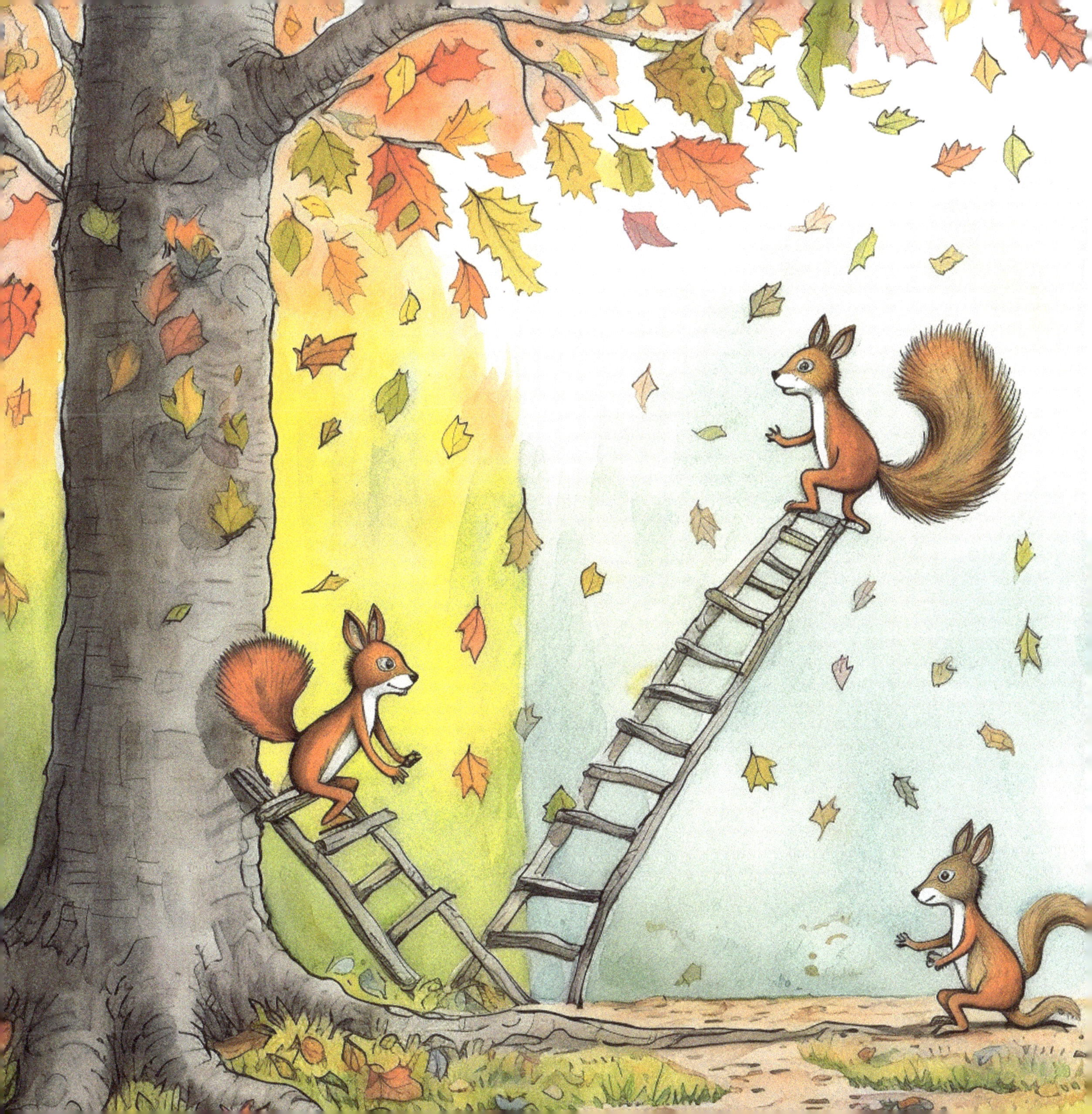

Teachers encourage us to
think critically,
ask questions,
and seek answers,
helping us become
lifelong learners.

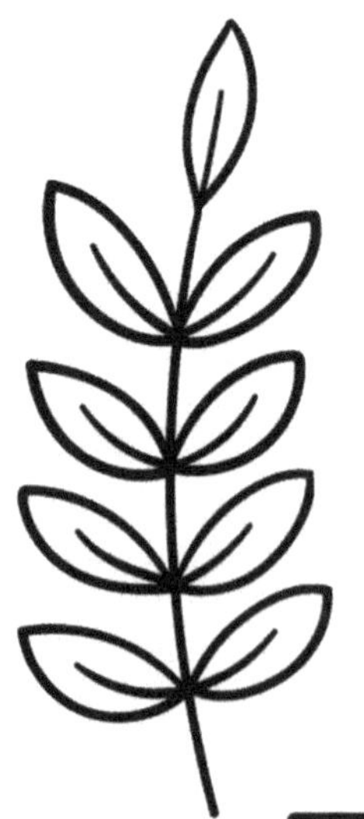

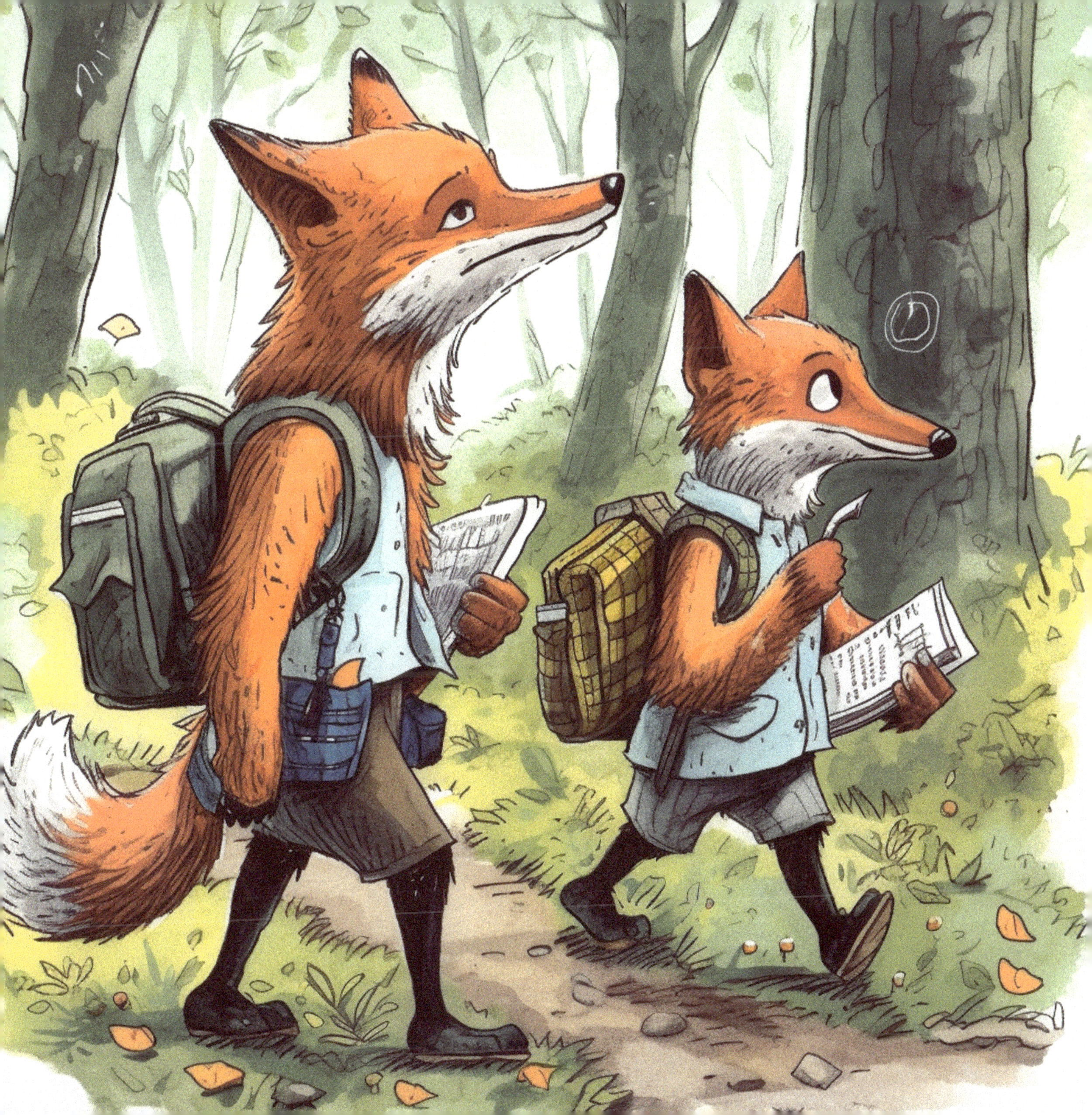

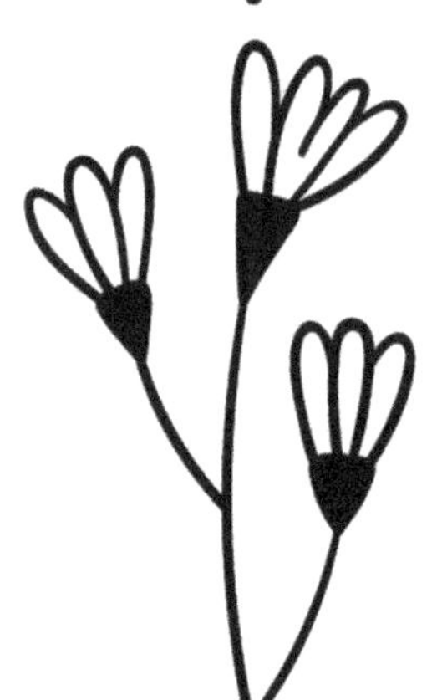

Through their guidance, teachers help us discover our strengths and talents, and give us the confidence to use them.

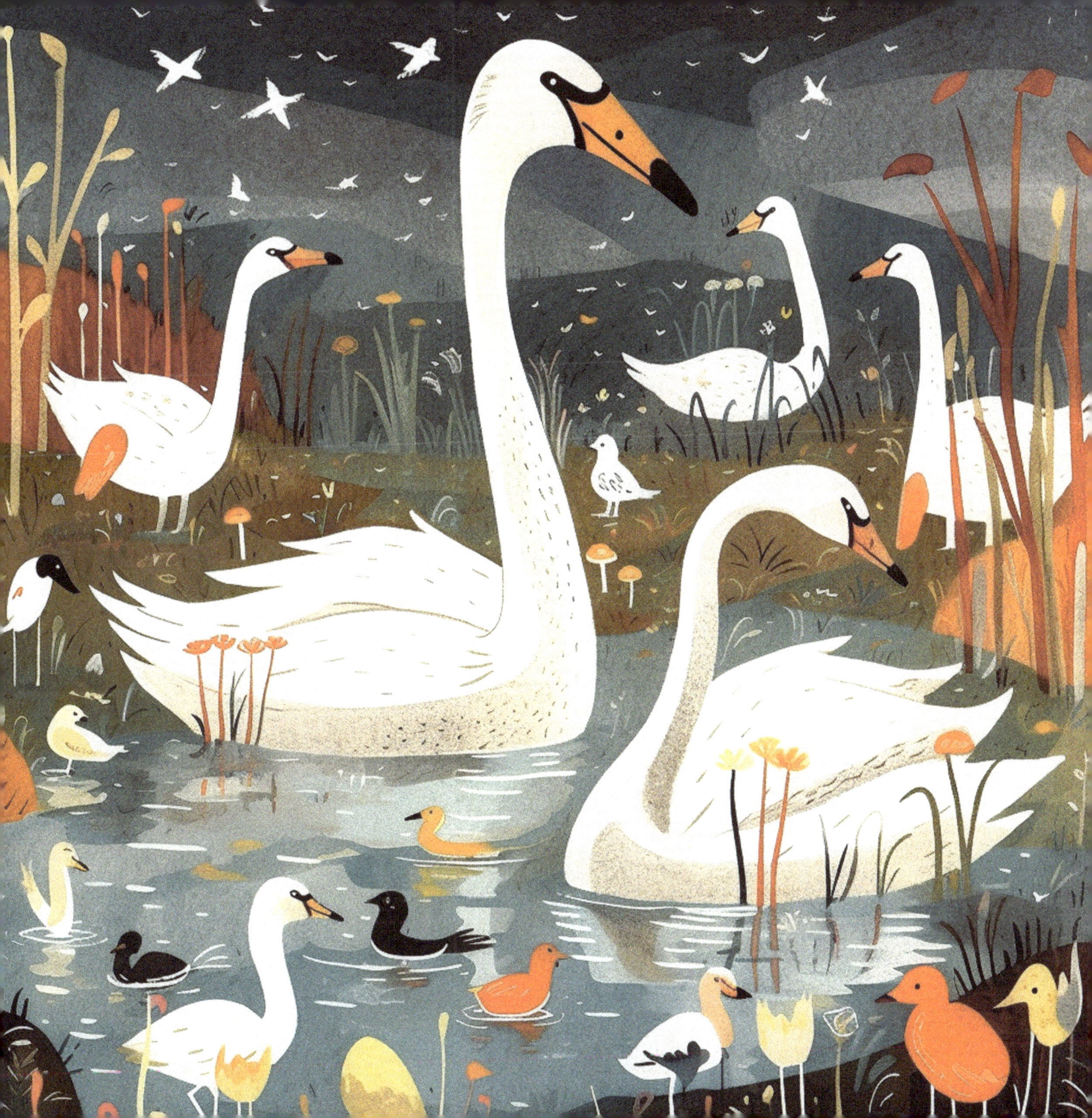

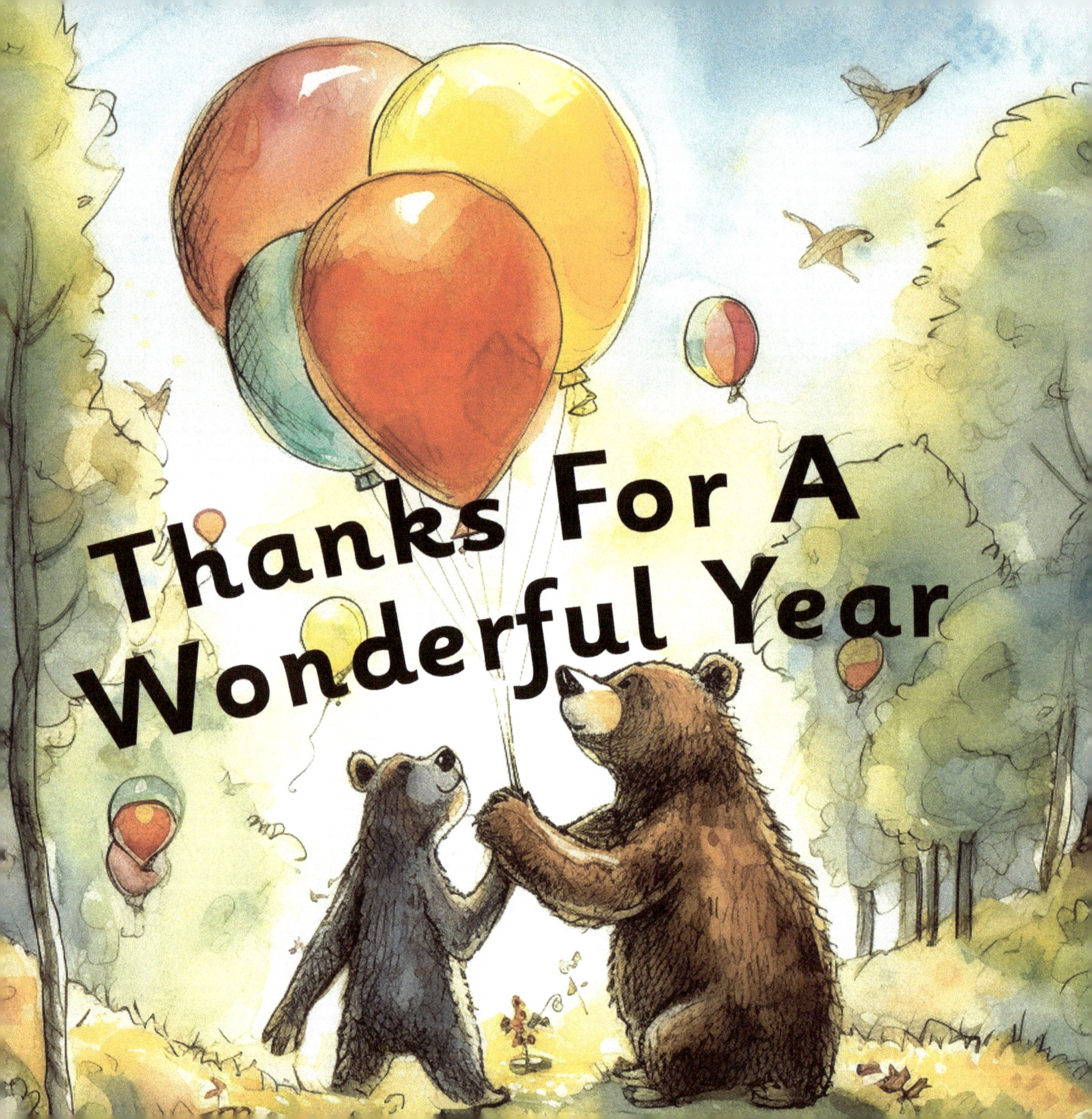

Thanks For A Wonderful Year